Animals Change

By Dennis Burns

Scott Foresman
is an imprint of

PEARSON

Glenview, Illinois • Boston, Massachusetts • Chandler, Arizona •
Upper Saddle River, New Jersey

Photographs

Every effort has been made to secure permission and provide appropriate credit for photographic material. The publisher deeply regrets any omission and pledges to correct errors called to its attention in subsequent editions.

Unless otherwise acknowledged, all photographs are the property of Pearson Education, Inc.

Photo locators denoted as follows: Top (T), Center (C), Bottom (B), Left (L), Right (R), Background (Bkgd)

Opener: GK & ©Vikki Har/Getty Images; **1** GK & ©Vikki Har/Getty Images; **3** (C) ©Gary Meszaros/Getty Images, (TR) ©William Osborn/Nature Picture Library; **4** ©Frank Lukasseck/Getty Images; **5** (TL) ©George McCarthy/Corbis, (C) ©Roger Tidman/Corbis; **6** ©Andy Rouse/Corbis; **7** AP Images/©AP Photo; **8** GK & Vikki Har/Getty Images.

ISBN 13: 978-0-328-46291-9
ISBN 10:   0-328-46291-8

Copyright © by Pearson Education, Inc., or its affiliates. All rights reserved. Printed in Mexico. This publication is protected by copyright, and permission should be obtained from the publisher prior to any prohibited reproduction, storage in a retrieval system, or transmission in any form or by any means, electronic, mechanical, photocopying, recording, or likewise. For information regarding permissions, write to Pearson Curriculum Rights & Permissions, One Lake Street, Upper Saddle River, New Jersey 07458.

Pearson® is a trademark, in the U.S. and/or in other countries, of Pearson plc or its affiliates.
Scott Foresman® is a trademark, in the U.S. and/or in other countries, of Pearson Education, Inc., or its affiliates.

A baby frog will change.

A baby bear will change.

A baby snake will change.

A baby lion will change.

A baby bird will change.

7

A baby dog will change.